V is for Victoria

By

Cheri Beatty

Dedication and Acknowledgment

I would like to dedicate this book to the Minnesota Boundary Waters and Quetico Wilderness area in Canada. I was introduced to this area when I was a young girl and it hooked me for life. Clear waters, dancing auroras, morning fog, campfires, and echoing midnight loon calls make this place a sanctuary like no other. A special thanks and acknowledgment to my papa Don for encouraging me to go on my first canoe trip and to my Grama Lorraine who taught me how to cook over a fire. My heart is grateful to my husband, John, for loving the wilderness with me and for being patient with our three kids in canoes over the years. To each of my children, I love that you are all carrying on the wilderness passion: Lake! And to our dear friend, Victoria, it was an honor to know you and imagine what you might have been capable of! Readers, I hope you love Victoria's story and enjoy many of the photo's in the book from the Boundary Waters area.

About the Author

Author of Suitcase Full of Horses, Just Wait, and V is for Victoria, Cheri Beatty is also a photographer, wife, dog-musher, mother of three humans, and many critters. Their family cabin in Ely, Minnesota is her favorite place to recharge and see God's hand in nature. This is where Cheri and her family were fortunate enough to meet Victoria.

V is for Victoria

Based on a true story.

A long time ago, a loon named Victoria
hatched all alone on a small island
in northern Minnesota.

Victoria grew up to be very strong and independent, but she never traveled too far from her island.

In those early days, the lakes were
full of garbage so not many birds
swam in the water.
Victoria was different though, she
loved to swim through the trash
and collect treasures.

Old bottles were Victoria's favorite to collect because when the wind blew over them, they whistled a lonesome melody. Since Victoria was often lonely, she liked the sound and often sang it back to the bottles.

On calm evenings, Canadian Geese flying overhead could hear the strange sound but they never got too close. Back then, geese only landed in Canada and loons always stayed in Minneosta.

One spring day, a strong wind blew
from the north and it began to rain
like it never had before!
Victoria did all she could do to protect
her treasures but she finally had to
dive into the water for shelter.

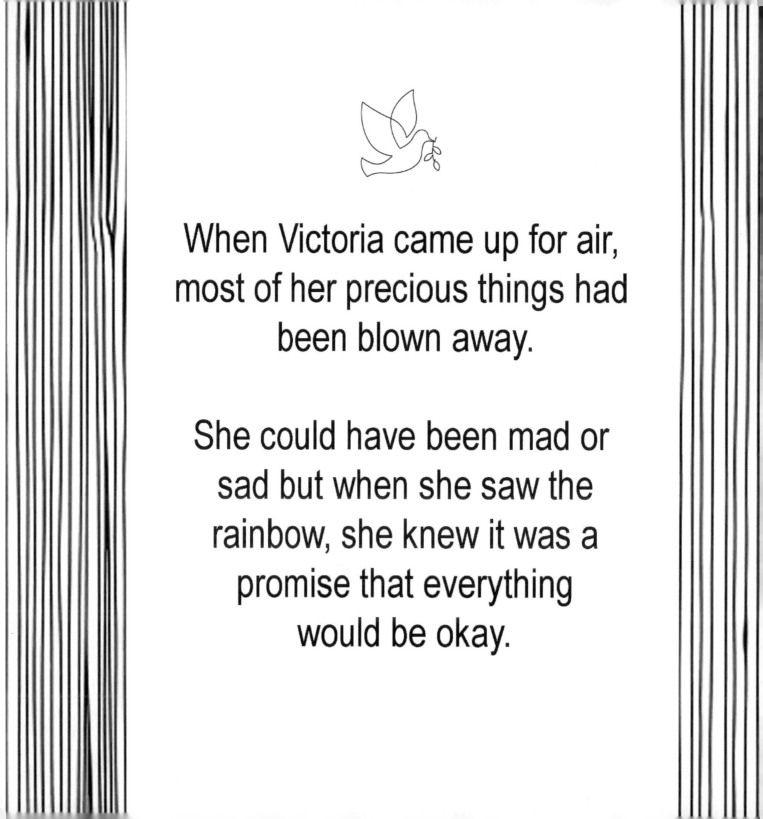

When Victoria came up for air,
most of her precious things had
been blown away.

She could have been mad or
sad but when she saw the
rainbow, she knew it was a
promise that everything
would be okay.

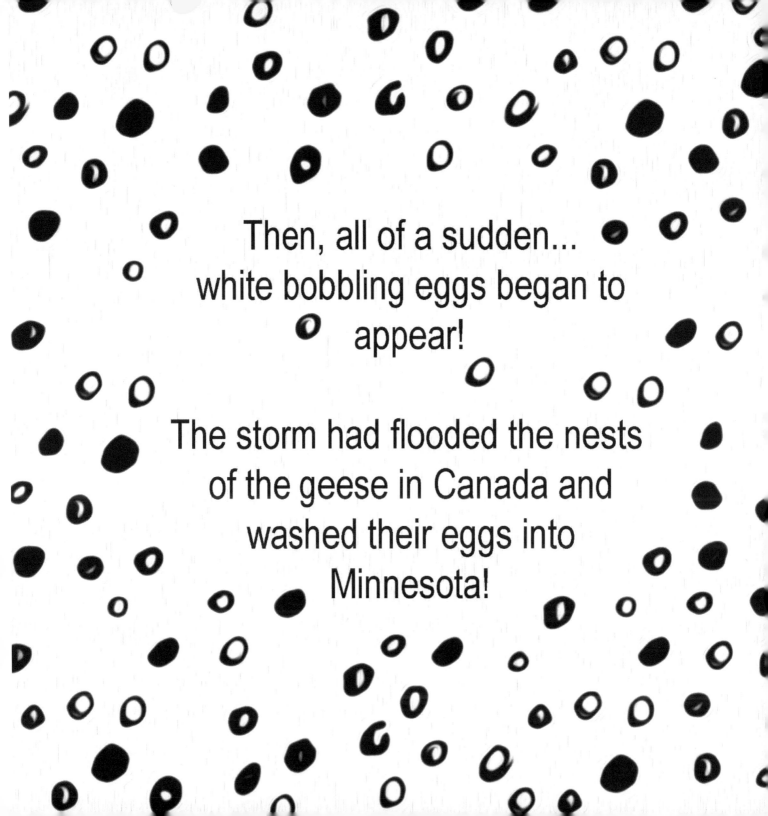

Then, all of a sudden...
white bobbling eggs began to
appear!

The storm had flooded the nests
of the geese in Canada and
washed their eggs into
Minnesota!

Quickly, Victoria gathered the eggs
every way she knew how!

Exhausted, she fell sound asleep
on a nest of eggs
(instead of bottles and bobbers)

Until...

CRACK, CRACK CRACK!!!

Hundreds of baby geese started
breaking out of their shells
and began crying!

Victoria, having never been a mother, didn't know what to do so she started singing the bottle song.

Immediately, the tiny geese calmed down and started chirping the tune back to Victoria!

When loons in the area heard the crying, they gathered in the middle of a lake to come up with a plan to find the parents of the little geese.

Boldly flying over the Canadian border,
the loons sang the bottle song.

The geese below remembered hearing
the same song from the strange little island!

Flocking to the island,
the parents found their babies
safe and happy!

The geese stayed with Victoria
until their babies were
strong enough to fly home.

Because the geese were so grateful to Victoria, they came up with an idea to do something special for her...

When it was time to say goodbye,
the geese all flew away in the
shape of a giant "V" for Victoria!

The geese promised to always
fly in V formation to honor
the loon who saved them.

Nearby campers were curious about the odd-flying geese so they ventured out to see what was happeing.

The people didn't understand what the geese and loons were doing but they were saddened to see all the trash in the water, so they began cleaning it up.

Victoria didn't miss her trash because she was too busy giving music lessons to loons and visiting with geese who stopped by to say hello.

Best of all,
Victoria was never lonely again.

Today, geese around the world still fly in V formation and other birds do now too! Loons have continued singing the lonely bottle song and if you see them gathering in the middle of the lake, know they're planning something big!

As for the lakes along the border between Canada and Minnesota, they remain some of the cleanest in the world.

Author's Notes about Victoria

On an island on Moose Lake in Ely, Minnesota, Victoria lived all alone. She sat on a nest full of old bobbers and whiskey bottles she had collected. One time, I tried to take the bobbers out of her nest so that she might leave and find a mate but she followed my paddle board until I returned the bobbers to her nest. She lived on that island for her entire life.

CPSIA information can be obtained
at www.ICGtesting.com
Printed in the USA
BVHW022155260922
648067BV00002B/6

9 781915 424990